WHISPERS OF A RESTLESS MIND

AALIYA KHAN

To the ones who feel too much,
Those who carry silent storms in their chest
and still rise.

To the dreamers, the overthinkers, the quiet rebels—
This book is for you.

And to everyone who ever made me believe in my words—
Thank you for whispering back when the world was loud.

Contents

Contents

Foreword

Poetry, at its core, is a quiet rebellion—soft yet sharp, subtle yet powerful. Whispers of a Restless Mind is a collection that doesn't scream for attention but instead leans in and speaks to the heart. These poems reflect the silent storms we endure, the healing we crave, and the courage it takes to feel deeply in a world that often asks us to numb ourselves.

As the author of this collection, I began writing not to be heard by many, but to be understood by even one. These verses are fragments of my own thoughts—some fragile, some fierce—all stitched together with honesty and hope.

I hope this book offers a mirror to those who seek comfort, clarity, or just the feeling that they are not alone. Whether you're flipping through these pages late at night or in the glow of a calm morning, I hope these whispers stay with you long after the final line.

Welcome to my restless mind. I'm glad you're here.

Preface

I never imagined I would be sharing these poems with people.

What began as scattered thoughts scribbled in notebooks, written in the margins of school notes or typed out quietly during emotional whirlwinds, slowly became something more—something real. As a young poet, writing has given me a voice, a way to explore and express what it means to grow, dream, and overcome. These words, born out of silent afternoons, late-night overthinking, and moments I didn't quite understand, started to form a rhythm. A voice. A home for everything I couldn't say out loud.

Whispers of a Restless Mind isn't just a poetry collection. It's a piece of me—a fragment of my heart pressed between paper. These pages carry quiet confessions, gentle rebellions, unspoken hopes, and truths I wish someone had told me when I needed to hear them most.

Each poem was written from a place of feeling. Sometimes that feeling was joy, but often it was confusion, hurt, uncertainty, or longing. And yet, poetry gave those feelings a shape, a name. It allowed me to unravel what I didn't even realise I was carrying.

This book is for those who've ever felt too much, too deeply. For those who overthink, who smile when they're crumbling inside, who hold space for others while forgetting to hold space for themselves. For the ones who love endlessly, who grieve quietly, who stay soft in a world that often demands hardness.

It's for the ones who are still finding their voice, and those who've just begun listening to it.

It's for you—if you've ever wondered whether your feelings were valid. They are.

If you've ever needed someone to say, "I get it." I do.

This book isn't here to provide answers. I won't pretend to have those. But it's taught me something important:

That even the softest whisper deserves to be heard.

That even unspoken pain deserves a language.

That healing doesn't always shout—it often comes in quiet, measured lines.

Writing this collection was my way of understanding myself. Sharing it is my way of reaching out to say you're not alone.

So, thank you. Thank you for picking up this book, for being curious enough to listen to a restless mind, for choosing to spend time inside these pages. I hope something here finds you exactly where you are. I hope one poem feels like a reflection. I hope another feels like a hand reaching back to hold yours.

And if nothing else, I hope you leave with a little more kindness toward yourself than when you arrived.

With deepest gratitude,

Aaliya

Acknowledgements

This book would never have existed without the gentle voices and strong hearts behind me.

To my parents, thank you for helping me see the potential I had long forgotten to believe in. Your quiet encouragement gave me the courage to keep writing even when I doubted myself.

To my teachers, thank you for reminding me that my words had weight and for pushing me to continue this journey when I needed it most.

To my dearest friends, thank you for always reading with patience, offering honest feedback, and cheering me on through every version, every draft, and every little line.

You all held me up when I was too afraid to speak.
Now this book speaks for me.

Forever grateful,

Aaliya

Prologue

Whispers of a Restless Mind is a heartfelt collection of poetry that delves into the intricacies of human emotions, self-reflection, resilience, and the complexities of modern life. Through evocative verses, this anthology explores themes of mental health, societal expectations, personal growth, and the beauty of nature.

The poems serve as an intimate window into the mind of a young poet, capturing unspoken emotions, quiet struggles, and fleeting moments of hope. With a raw and introspective tone, each piece invites readers to connect with their own inner world and find solace in shared experiences.

This collection is a journey—one that embraces vulnerability, celebrates strength, and reminds us all of the power of words to heal and inspire. Written with a deep sense of awareness and emotion, *Whispers of a Restless Mind* offers a unique perspective that resonates with readers across all walks of life.

1. HARMONY BEYOND THE NOISE

Surrounded by the clamour of the world,
We find the peace within.
Thoughts of worldly matters in our minds swirled,
Thinking about ourselves once feels like a societal sin.
People will give their verdict,
No matter the perseverance and resilience put in.
Be positive and avoid the inner conflict,
Or in the never-ending cycle of society-pleasing, you'll spin.
Take a moment to reflect on yourself,
You're your best version, you will soon believe.
Don't let the thoughts get to you of self-disbelief,
Inner peace will be what you achieve!

2. WARS, VIOLENCE AND CHAOS

I felt delighted to be born,
In this world blessed with every resource.
But now I feel everyone mourns,
Cries, Fades and is with an expression so morose.
My world has been scattered with endless wars,
Which has left everyone in great shock.
Mankind has become selfish and it is the cause,
Now people don't take an initiative and just mock.
It is such a disappointment to see,
How we all lost our values because of power and greed.
How sad it seems to me,
For those who are trapped in the cruel mankind's deeds.
Dear God bless thy world,
Which you created for us to enrich.
This land is now getting cursed,
With wars and riots on a high pitch.

3. THERE WILL COME A DAY

There will come a day,
When I have a voice full of puissance.
And I wish I may,
Fly away with confidence.
There will come a day,
When there'll be no bird in a cage locked.
And I wish they may,
Fly away in a beautiful flock.
There will come a day,
When there will be no one pressurised.
And I wish they may,
Fly away when by all they will be recognised.
There will come a day,
When there will be no problems at all.
And I wish we all may,
Fly away somewhere where there is nothing to solve.

4. A THOUGHT

My mind is full of thoughts,
But no one's there to listen.
They say I've become quiet,
But do we ever try to make the burden lessen?
"People will always be on my side"
I used to believe.
During times of need, they hide,
Only hopelessness is what I receive.
I've seen my dreams shatter,
Full of love and desire.
"Do I matter?"
A question that inside me starts up a fire.
Happiness in solitude, I tried to discover,
Which I believed would bring skills to me in mass.
However, no matter how much pain I try to cover,
My throat hurts as if stabbed by pieces of glass.
I may not be sensitive,
I may not be weak.
I just carry a different perspective,
And a little love and respect that I seek.

5. I AM PERFECTION

Hand me a mirror,
I'll try to find pulchritude.
I may have flaws but I'm not a quitter,
For me, that's the right attitude.
If the time is intolerable,
I am unbreakable enough to handle.
I'm myself and incomparable,
Of pride and resilience, I carry a candle.
It's not only about me but you as well,
For once let's look upon ourselves with eyes of love.
Let's make our body where a soul of content dwells,
And with realization of self-worth, our head rises above.

6. WILL I BE FINE?

My heart feels heavy,
Too many feelings to bear.
Though I'm surrounded by a bevvy,
No one's there to hear.
Wish people were empathetic,
It'll forever remain a dream.
People should not be that pathetic,
My inner voices scream.
It's alright and I'll take my time,
To grow from the failures and misjudgements.
I'll try not to care, and I might get fine,
But identify if that's my true sentiment.

7. IT'S JUST ME…

I feel a sense of guilt pounding inside me,
Uncertain if I'm even enough.
I want the heavy thoughts to set me free,
Can't handle this, but trying to be tough.
Self-belief is something I have completely,
In the past few battles of thoughts inside me.
Mental peace for me holds a high cost,
Try constantly, but can't move ahead.
It's hard to impress others,
No matter how hard one tries.
I keep everything to myself, and not even a single word I utter,
Yet my nights are full of my silent cries.

8. THE CONFIDENCE ANTHEM

Words of discouragement pound,
But you never gave up.
Mental strength is what you've found,
You keep going ahead and up.
You're your own therapist,
You now believe.
Took a step back from being conformist,
Now greatness is what you achieve.
Keep moving on with the same confidence,
Everyone will soon feel proud.
All that worked out was your perseverance,
Now hear the applause getting loud.

9. 'OVER'- Everything

Am I really a person worth living,
Or I'm just here to suffer?
Should I brush off this feeling?
And try becoming tougher.
Sometimes, I just want to give up,
On my dreams, hopes and everything.
Should I try to speed up?
And pull all the unpulled strings.
I can't stop this load on my head,
It's increasing day by day,
I know I may end up in dread,
When all the bad memories replay.
I feel as if I'm worthless and undeserving,
And that might be true.
Hopelessness inside me is burning,
It's something that only I can view.
Everything now seems temporary,
Can you help me prove it wrong?
It's not that possible or necessary,
But if you can, then how?

10. TENSION, TRAUMA AND TABOOS

The youth is challenging enough,
But still, mental health degrades.
We are told to be "rough and tough",
But what about when gossip trades?
Taboos have dominated society,
Reformations need to be brought.
Why have we youngsters stopped taking things lightly?
Is it our rigid society or our mind full of thoughts?
Early-age trauma has affected many,
Leaving youngsters heavy-headed.
We see them go through a selfish bully's deeds,
When their innocence is used and rented.

11. WHAT A DAY IT WAS~

What a day it was,
When I got to admire the beautiful nature.
No borders and no laws,
A perfect theme for relaxation and literature.
Peace was my state of mind then,
When I sat down with zest.
With a book and a pen,
Looking at the alluring scene, I was writing my best.
Birds are chirping and flying everywhere,
Making the scene even more divine.
I get all my joy just by a touch that's mere,
Which makes me forget all sputters of mine.

12. A DAY IN SUMMER!

A simple normal day,
Where I'm busy with my own sputters.
The sun is setting in its own way,
On these days of summer.
When I step out,
I see some sort of magnificence in the skies.
Children in excitement shout,
The butterflies dance, flutter and flies.
I picked up a chair and sat comfortably,
The sun is setting down alluringly.
I kept looking at the colourful skies continuously,
And enjoyed the moment's delicacy.
All my troubles I forgot at once,
Looking at a fine piece of art by nature.
Now, I just see the gift of nature and the things it has done,
I bet this sunset was enjoyed by every creature!

13. A NIGHT TO NEVER FORGET

Tonight, the stars seem a bit different,
They're appearing more angelic to me.
The night sky tonight has a divine scent,
That attracts me.
I got out of these echo chambers,
Just to admire the delicacy.
I look above, and the night sky takes me further,
To the admirable hills and seas.
I sat down, satisfied by the stars,
Enjoying the shooting stars is yet another experience.
I wasn't bored sitting for hours,
Tonight wasn't just great, it also made me feel delirious.

14. HOW NATURE CAUGHT MY EYE

I am going down the woodland,
Inspired by the pulchritude.
Butterflies come and sit on my hand,
With elegance and attitude.
Flowers, trees and fragrance,
Are somehow making me feel gleeful.
The way with the breeze the flowers dance,
It looks so beautiful.
How does it even feel waking up in the lap of nature,
The birds dance splendidly.
They are such beautiful creatures,
Other birds also join them with joy and glee.
I don't want to leave this place,
I admire it a lot.
It feels great to see animals doing things in different ways,
Such beautiful sights in the camera of my eyes I have caught!

15. THE WAY I LOVE YOU

You are my Sun if I'm the sunflower,
Always leaning towards you.
You're my strength and ultimate power,
People like you are very few.
Holding me in your embrace,
Was always like a balm to my soul,
If I had to choose someone with unmatched grace.
I can't forget your role.
Count the stars in the sky tonight,
Possibly infinite In number.
My love for you is no less or light,
It's so profound that even the stars it will outnumber!

16. THE UNSPOKEN WORDS I HIDE

Feelings of emptiness dominate my mind,
Unsure of my next steps.
Strength and peace are things I can no longer find,
Struggling with the depth.
My heart is loaded with gallons of feelings,
Just need an ear and embrace.
I can feel the abysmal thoughts creeping,
And the darkness that surrounds me in solace.
Misapprehensions build up the tension,
Making the silent cries grow in my head.
Waiting for the unjustified emotions to lose their retention,
But there is always meaning behind something which embeds.
Just because I bury my feelings,
Under the veil of my face and my heart.
It doesn't mean I'm easily healing,
With all the pain that doesn't effortlessly depart.

17. HERE COMES THE RAIN

Such pleasant sounds,
Such pleasant views.
When the refreshing fragrance of grass abounds,
And looking at the sky's grey and white hues.
The winds and the drops of water,
Are somehow making me feel gleeful.
A great opportunity to write a poem for an author,
Which captures the scene which can be the most beautiful.
The thundering lights roar like a brave Lion,
In the dark night skies.
Our surroundings go silent,
When the storm starts getting violent.

18. WE ALL HAVE A TALENT

A bird cannot fly on its first try
But nobody saw the bird cry,
Humans are the same
Just that they gained a little more fame.
Many of us believe,
Just on the first try, there should be a task that we perceive
At School, children bully a kid,
But they don't know in that kid what Talent could be hid.
At the Office, the Boss scolds the man,
Rather than saying "You can"
Why don't we come together,
Abolish this bullying forever.
Don't sit silent,
Just show them your talent
Not all of us are the same,
But in our way we can gain the fame.

19. THE BITTER TRUTHS

A world full of varied outlooks you're surrounded with,
Expectant eyes looking for downfalls.
Societal support is a confirmed obvious myth,
Understanding stands in between, like an enormous wall.
Expressing opposition is treated as a felony,
Only contributing to rage and agitation.
Pressure so extreme that raises agony,
Thoughts in our mind cause commotion.
These are some bitter truths we often close our eyes to,
Even though it leaves a cavernous impact.
The effect is something only we can view,
No matter what we do, this ugly pain always attracts.

20. WE'LL GROW THROUGH IT ALL

See the world through our eyes,
It'll appear dismal and bleak.
Maybe it's just our inner power we need to realize,
To create a world full of hope and faith, we seek.
None of us are alone in this quest of ecstasy,
Still mounting from the clutches of petrifying brainwaves.
Striving to attain spiritual harmony endlessly,
Like a perpetual mark, a stone engraves.
Bond ourselves together like an unbreakable chain,
Nothing can stop us from being optimistic.
No mighty power or force can ever cause us pain,
With the conviction of becoming dominant and idealistic.

21. WHY US?

Silent cries fill up the emptiness,
Heart and Head are not ready for this crisis.
Where are all those cherished moments of happiness?
Were heartbreaks already a part of our lives thesis?
Certainty has lost its way in this dread of emotions,
Leaving melancholy and mayhem behind.
Struggling to move forward with an unexplainable kind of
confusion,
Fear of fiasco is consuming the rationality of my mind.
It's like a road that never comes to an end,
Making you endure the worst scenarios ever imagined.
The everlasting scars in my heart could never be mended,
Maybe the miseries in my fate were predestined.
Isn't it amusing that tender hearts always get broken first?
Maybe everyone likes a little playful banter with us.
It's just that the little hope that has kept us immersed,
Because these constant despairs are turning us wuss.

22. IT WILL BE ALRIGHT

It's the wound that will forever bleed.
Filling me up with feelings of discontent.
Soon, I realised, reassurance was what I need,
With which in life I can ascend.
The pieces of my heart may come in form again,
Only if I continue to stay positive.
I'm trying my utmost to wash away the pain,
And about the worst, I will no longer be inquisitive.
The ocean waves of optimism will wash away the marks,
Leaving my heart rejuvenated.
With a candle of hope and faith, I will light up the dark,
Proud of the fresh mindset I created.

23. JUST LET GO

My heart is equivalent to a crumbled piece of paper,
The scars have always been there.
The daunting words turning my confidence into vapor,
Making me lose belief in love and care.
Things don't always go our way,
Making us lose forbearance.
We keep it to ourselves, and nothing we say,
But at times of uncertainty, we do need assurance.
Heart is tender like a flower,
But head turning into a piece of stone.
Pain will lose retention hour by hour,
The day we reach our milestones.

24. A PLEA TO PAIN

Dear pain, am I that treasured for you?
That it's always me who gets shattered first.
Am I that deserving of you?
I'm like a necessity, but nothing is worth more than dust.
Dear pain, will I always be the one to care?
During times of hardship, there's no one for me.
Will there always be no one there?
Who can stand as a pillar of support for me?
Dear pain, why, at times, are you so unfair?
That you first break the benevolent.
With whom can I the moments of gloom share?
Life no longer seems succulent.
Dear pain, can we have an agreement for once?
That you will spare me and myself from shattering.
Will you still consider me a dunce?
If I give up on this one to save this from people's chattering.

25. A FLICKER IN DARKNESS

A rose growing through a bush of thorns,
Full of taunts and words of dismay.
Through all the obstacles, a resilient soul is born,
Within the crowd of taboos, we find our way.
Shining like the only star in a cloudy night sky,
Like the one who lasted the tough times.
Find answers within yourself when life slams a "why?",
Because being doting on yourself is no crime.
You put yourself together when a spark of pride is inflicted,
Pushing you to come out of your state of ignorance.
When your mindset shifted,
You provided yourself with control and clearance.

26. ECHOES OF REGRET

Not at all times does strength work,
At times, endeavours go unawarded.
For some success still lurks,
Accepting in life what's accorded.
Sometimes it makes me feel numb,
Over the multiple times I've failed.
Is life trying to prove I am unworthy and dumb?
Towards content, my ship never sailed.
Daunting words trap my soul,
Surrounded by echo chambers of regrets.
To escape is now my only goal,
I'm tired of treating fiascos as my secrets.

27. UNCERTAINTES

Lost the glint of fortitude in my eyes,
Now, tranquillity is what I seek.
Puissance; out of the cage, it flies,
Endeavours falling, lifeless and weak.
Clouds of confusion make it hazy to see,
Towards which direction does my ship sail?
Contemplation of thoughts never set me free,
Shadow of pain behind me; trails.
Freedom from this cage is all I crave,
Where echo chambers of daunting words I'm surrounded with.
Forbid me from carrying this suffering to my grave,
Don't prove peace in my life as a myth.

28. SHE

She looks brave to you on the face,
But inside, she is shattered.
Thoughts on her race,
For her, she never mattered.
Caught in a whirl of emotions,
She'll stand for one another.
Selflessness, she carries as her central notion,
Not a single word for herself she'll ever utter.
Put on a veil to hide her pain,
Cause her thoughts were never invited.
Now, she cries under the rain,
Because she chose to get selflessness inside her lightened.
Always there on the other's side to empathise,
But killed herself inside; no reassurance.
Through the adversities, she would rise,
And would may also learn to provide her assurance.

29. OH, THE SOCIETY!

They say I should talk more,
And share pieces of myself with them.
Oblivious to the fact that they broke me to the core,
Switching roles just doesn't suit them.
I suppressed my voices and cries,
Or else they'll label me as 'sensitive'.
Glued a fake smile and blurted beautiful lies,
Forgot what a real smile was; feels negative.
Constant eyes surround me,
Hungrily looking for flaws.
Optimism, like a bird, it flees,
Now anxiety towards me, creeps and crawls.

About The Author

Aaliya Khan (born in 2011) is a young poet with a deep passion for words and storytelling. Writing has been her sanctuary, allowing her to explore emotions, self-reflection, and the complexities of the world around her. Her poetry delves into themes of mental resilience, self-acceptance, societal expectations, and the beauty of nature, creating a space where readers can find solace and inspiration.

As an aspiring writer, Aaliya aims to use poetry as a medium to connect with others, offering both introspection and hope through her verses. *Whispers of a Restless Mind* is her debut poetry collection, capturing the raw emotions and thoughts of a restless yet thoughtful soul.

When not writing, Aaliya enjoys immersing herself in literature, music, and the endless inspiration the world offers.

Readers can reach out to her at: aaliyakhan7931@gmail.com — she'd love to hear your thoughts!

www.ingramcontent.com/pod-product-compliance
Lightning Source LLC
Chambersburg PA
CBHW031247130726
47988CB00008B/3277